Library of Congress Cataloging-in-Publication Data

Watts, Barrie.
  Birds' nest.

    (Stopwatch books)
    Includes index.
    Summary: Photographs, drawings, and text on
two levels of difficulty examine the characteristics
of a blue tit family as the male and female build
a nest, mate, and care for their young.
    1. Blue tit — Juvenile literature. [1. Blue
tit. 2. Birds] I. Title. II. Series.
  QL696.P2615W38 1987   598.8'24   86-31457
  ISBN 0-382-09443-3
  ISBN 0-382-09439-5 (lib. bdg.)

First published by A & C Black (Publishers) Limited
35 Bedford Row, London WC1R 4JH

© 1986 Barrie Watts

Published in the United States in 1987
by Silver Burdett Press,
Englewood Cliffs, New Jersey.

Acknowledgements
The artwork is by Helen Senior
The publishers would like to thank Jean Imrie for her help and advice.

Birds' nest

Barrie Watts

Silver Burdett Press • Englewood Cliffs, New Jersey

Here is a blue titmouse.

The blue titmouse lives in many countries in Europe. They make their homes in parks and gardens. In summer they eat caterpillars and insects. In winter they might come to bird feeders for scraps of food.

This blue titmouse is eating peanuts at a bird feeder.

Soon the blue titmouse will find a mate. When spring comes, they will both look for a place to build a nest and have their young.

This book will tell you how a blue titmouse family grows up.

The birds look for a place to build a nest.

The birds must find a safe, dry place to build their nest. Some blue titmice make their nests in holes in trees or walls. These birds have found a nesting box in someone's garden.

Look at the photograph. The female bird is looking inside the nesting box. The round hole is the only way to get in and out of the box. It will be a safe place to build a nest.

The birds build a nest.

The birds collect grass and moss to build their nest.
They carry it in their beaks back to the nesting box.
Then they arrange the grass into a nest.

Look at the big photograph. The female bird has
brought some hair and feathers to make the inside of
the nest soft and warm.

When the nest is finished, the blue titmice will mate.

The female lays her eggs.

The female mates with the male many times.
Then she can start to lay her eggs. The eggs are very
small. Here is one next to a hen's egg.

Each morning, the female lays one egg. Then she flies
away. At night she comes back to the nest to sleep, and
the next day she lays another egg.

Look at the big photograph. How many eggs has the female
laid in her nest? Blue titmice usually lay between seven and
fourteen eggs.

The blue titmouse keeps her eggs warm.

When the female has laid all her eggs, she sits
on them to keep them warm. She keeps moving them around
to make sure that each one is warm all over. If the eggs
get cold they will not hatch.

The female bird has to sit on her eggs all day.
She does not often fetch her own food. The male bird
brings food to the nest for her.

The birds hatch from the eggs.

After twelve days the birds hatch from the eggs.
They are very hungry and they open their beaks wide
to ask for food.

These tiny birds are only one day old.

When the young birds hatch, they have no feathers and
cannot open their eyes. Each one is only as long as a pin.

Look at the big photograph. The young birds are now a
week old.

The young birds are always hungry.

Each young bird needs to eat over a hundred insects and caterpillars a day! The parents take turns feeding their young. Every few minutes they have to bring more food to the nest.

The young birds are now ten days old. They can open their eyes and they are beginning to grow feathers. First they grow quills, which are like short, hard straws. You can see them in the photograph. Then feathers start to grow from the quills.

The blue titmice keep their nest clean.

The blue titmice must keep their nest clean. If it gets dirty the young birds could become ill.

Look at the photograph. The young blue titmouse is letting the male pull out its dropping.

The parents take away all the droppings and drop them on the ground away from the nest.

The young birds grow fast.

Now the young birds are fifteen days old.

Their eyes are wide open and they have grown soft gray and yellow feathers. They will not grow their adult feathers until the autumn.

The young birds are nearly as big as their mother and father. They still need to be fed by their parents.

The young birds get ready to leave the nest.

Soon the young birds start to explore the nesting box.
Look at the photograph. The blue titmice are nineteen days old.
They are fully grown and soon they will leave the nest.

This young bird is stretching its wings. It is ready to fly.

The young birds learn how to fly.

On a warm sunny day, the birds fly out of the nest.
This young bird has just flown for the first time.
It is tired so it is taking a rest on a branch.

The parent birds feed their young for three more
weeks. Then the young birds will have to find their own
food. They will leave their parents and fly away.

Next year the young blue titmice will look for somewhere to
build a nest. What do you think will happen in the nest?

Do you remember what happens in a nest?
See if you can tell the story in your own words.
You can use these pictures to help you.

1

2

4

5

3

6

Index

This index will help you to find some of the important words in the book.

If you want birds to visit you, hang some unsalted peanuts outside in a string bag. Remember to put them in a safe, sheltered place.